A Teen's Guide to Succeed in High School

Setting and Achieving your Goals

Monique Lynelle

A Teen's Guide To Succeed in High School

By: Monique Lynelle

Published by

Monique Lynelle

A Teen's Guide to Succeed in High School ©2012, Monique Lynelle. All rights reserved. No part of this book may be produced in any form or by any means including electronic, mechanical or photo-copying or stored in a retrieval system without permission in writing from the publisher except by a reviewer who may quote brief passages to be included in a review.

Find more info at www.MoniqueLynelle.com

Table of Contents

Pre-High School

Chapter 1 - 9th grade

New School – Don't Panic

Join Organizations

Chapter 2 - 10th grade

Concentrate on your education

Don't Do Drugs!

Chapter 3 - 11th grade

Prepare for your Next Step

Don't Be a Bully

Chapter 4 - 12th grade

Think about your future

The End of the Road

Pre-High School

  Before High School there are a few things you should consider. One important thing you should think about pertains to choosing a career. Where would you like to go to college? If you even want to attend college directly after High School. It is not too soon to decide, even if you change your mind later. By deciding on a career before entering High School, one can know whether they want to attend a vocational school, a performing arts school, a college prep program or even join the ROTC program; which will prepare you for the military after High School. Don't be afraid to ask your parents about the schools in your area that peek your interest. You have to apply to High Schools or have an idea of which High School program you would like to attend when you are in 7th and 8th grade. Your future does depend on the decisions you make now. People might tell you that you are too young to know what you want, but sometimes you have to take chances; and investing in yourself, along with your future is the best thing you can do as a teenager. Have fun being young. If you can take a career assessment test then that might help you understand your strengths and weaknesses. If you are not ready to decide on a career just yet, then don't, find out more about yourself and what you like and then choose a career.

Goals for High School

Short Term Goals

1. _____

   _____

   _____

   _____

   _____

   _____

   _____

2. _____

   _____

   _____

   _____

   _____

   _____

   _____

3. _____
   _____
   _____
   _____
   _____
   _____
   _____

Long Term Goals

1. _____
   _____
   _____
   _____
   _____
   _____
   _____

2. _____
   _____
   _____
   _____
   _____
   _____
   _____
   _____

3. _____
   _____
   _____
   _____
   _____
   _____
   _____
   _____
   _____

Chapter 1 - 9th Grade

New School – Don't Panic

There are times in everyone's life when they are the new person or something is new to them. High School is no different. The main reason to attend school is to learn. During this time in your life, peer pressure could be an issue. Regardless of your home situation, you can take responsibility for your own actions; and make good decisions as a teenager.

Speaking of choices, when I was in High School I moved around and ended up at four different High Schools, not by choice, but because my parents moved around quite a bit during my High School years. The friendships I could have built by staying in one school for four years didn't happen because of the moves. Also, I moved to four different states; from Philadelphia, PA, to Bloomfield, CT, to Hyattsville, MD, and to Kaneohe HI. I was so distracted and tired of moving, I ended up getting married before my last year in High School and moved away. I am not saying it is wrong to get married, but I do think getting your education is more important during your High School years than being in an intimate relationship. Engaging in adult activities as a teen can sometimes complicate matters. I know from experience and I just wanted to share one of my choices.

Now back to you all, making smart solid decisions can help you in the future. Try to stay focused on your assignments and go on outings with friends, teammates, and associates. Start looking into organizations that interest you and inquire about joining them. If you never played an instrument and you are interested; then try it. If you want to play a sport, then try out for a team. If you want to dance or be a cheer leader then try out. If you have to attend a school that does not have the extra-curricular activity you want to participate in, then look for programs in your community. There are places like the "YMCA," and "Freedom Theatre," in Philadelphia; some churches have excellent programs, dance, step teams, plays or choirs, but so do community centers or "boys and girls clubs." Sometimes you have to show interest and tell your parents or your guardian what interest you. Remember, you are important and you will be a future leader in this country, so what you do does matter and you have to believe that. Have pride in yourself and in your appearance, but stay humble and respectful of others. Use good hygiene and take care of yourself, you are old enough now to wash your own clothes, shower, and brush your teeth, comb or brush your hair to look presentable. It is time to grow up without being a grown up, but remember you can still have fun just being you, your age, with your peers. You will have the rest of your life to have a job and pay bills, so now is the time to meet new people, be friendly, not a push-over and learn some things about yourself. Believe me, it is better to learn what you would like to do now, rather than wait until your 50 years old to try to figure it out. Start planning now.

Join Organizations

As I mentioned earlier, find some things you are interested in and try to find an organization that will fit your swagger. If you are not into instruments, sports or cheer leading, you might want to join the student government or be a peer mediator. In 9th grade, you might not be able to join some organizations yet, but it is not too early to show interest in a group and prepare yourself to be a part of it in the future.

Observe your surroundings and look at people's character before you get extremely close to them in school. Although some people want to learn and make new friends; other kids are just bad news. Some teens gravitate to people with strong personalities, which they might need to help them deal with their issues. Your job is not to be someone's babysitter that is the same age as you, but if you happen to know someone is doing the wrong thing and you are their friend or you think they are cool, be smart and say that's not right. Sometimes you will have to leave where you are and get help, don't stick around and get in trouble for another person's mistake or bad choice.

Try not to have sex as long as you can before you get married. I know people slip up and make mistakes, but think about your future before you give your body to someone else. It is harder to stop having sex once you've already started having sex. Some people preach abstinence, and I think that is the best way to keep a clear head and make some good decisions regarding your future, but things do not always happen that way. Realistically, some teens have sex before they graduate High School and it really does not make life's decisions any easier. Just hear me out on this issue. Think of your body as a special gift and it cost a whole lot of money, better yet it is priceless, which means no amount of money is enough to buy it. If you would not buy the person you plan on giving your body to, an expensive present, then you don't need to have sex with them. It's not worth it. Your body is that present and you should love someone and care about them and hopefully be married to them before you give your present away; because once it's gone you cannot ever get it back. There are no refunds or exchanges on your body. If your parents allow you to go out, go in groups and keep your clothes on at all times. Go in the restroom stalls by yourself, stay away from watching movies at each other's house alone with the lights dim. Turn on all the lights until your outside and then don't sit too close, keep your hands to yourself. Now that you've got that, you are ready for the next school year.

Don't Be a Bully

    Don't do things to other people that you would not want them to do to you. If you know someone's secret and it is not causing trouble or bringing harm to anyone, then do not tell their personal business. If you want people to respect you, then you should respect them first. If you are a leader, then don't follow the crowd doing the wrong thing. If you are not sure that something is wrong, then stop, and think if you would want someone to treat you that way. Really, this is a simple thing to do, but people think they are stronger when they are in a group, but really it takes strength to stand on your own and do the right thing. Sometimes that is what it takes to be a leader. You are old enough by now to know right from wrong and make choices, so do the right thing. Don't pick on the new person or someone that is different from you just because they are different. That doesn't mean to just follow behind people, just because they are different either; it just means that respecting others for being human, like you; is the right thing to do. Sometimes someone might try to bully you and you might have to defend yourself, don't be afraid to stand up for yourself. Remember everyone will not read this book, or have parents telling them right from wrong. My advice is to defend yourself against a bully and then get help from an authority figure that will hopefully help smooth out the situation. Do not sit there and get bullied every day, because that is a problem also. You do not have to be a victim just because you are not the bully. Being a victim is not cool either. Stand up for yourself, respect yourself and others.

Short Term Goals

1.

_____

_____

_____

_____

_____

_____

2.

_____

_____

_____

_____

_____

3.

_____

_____

_____

_____

_____

_____

_____

_____

_____

Long Term Goals

1.

_____

_____

_____

_____

2.

3.

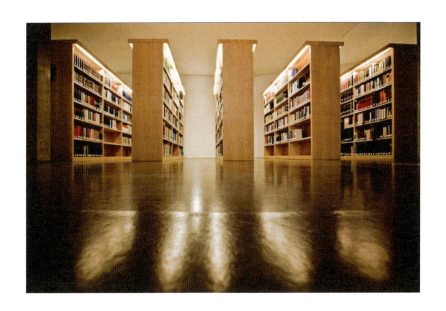

Chapter 2 - 10th Grade

Concentrate on Your Education

Concentrate on your education and your social programs. This year have fun but make sure your grades are on point. If you are having trouble at home, go to your guidance counselor or ask someone for help. If you are not doing well in a subject that you know you need to pass, like English or Math, then ask someone at school or your teacher for a tutor. If the school does not have a tutoring program then ask another student that is doing well in that class to help you with that subject. It is better to ask than to end up with a bad grade.

Don't give up because of home situations; remember you need to finish High School to go into a career later in life, not just to have a job. Everyone deserves a good education, regardless of the neighborhood they live in. Everyone should have a chance to learn. If you don't like your school or you want to be in a different program, decide now because it is better to transfer before your junior year.

Don't Do Drugs!

Drugs will not help you achieve your goals. Don't be a victim to peer pressure, rape, jail or anything else because you think it might be fun to try drugs. Later in life you might suffer from your decision to take drugs now. Some drugs have long term affects and some stay in your system longer than others. Drugs can kill you or ruin your life forever. Be careful around friends that are taking drugs and get help for them if you know they are using drugs. Some people want to escape from their problems and do not care at the moment about what they are doing to themselves. Some people just need someone to talk to that can help them deal with an issue. Be smart about it, and talk to someone if you need help. You'd be surprised at who might help you if you just reach out for help. There are counselors and group therapy sessions that can help you sort out your issues, and ultimately help you make wise decisions for your future.

Short Term Goals

1.

_____

_____

_____

_____

_____

_____

2.

_____

_____

_____

_____

_____

3.

Long Term Goals

1.

2.

3.

Chapter 3 - 11th grade

Prepare for your Next Step

By the end of this school year, you should know if you want to go into the military, go to college or go into a vocation. This year is the time to make sure you pay attention in class and do your best. Don't get side tracked with anything else, make school a priority and then have fun. When you know that doing well in school will ensure a brighter future, for yourself; it will motivate you to do what you have to do to excel in life.

Start looking at what Colleges or University's you are interested in, or which branch of the service you are interested in, or even which vocational school you would like to attend after High School. These things are important to look into now, so you can have a clear plan by your senior year. This would be a good time to discuss options with parents or guardians concerning your next step in life. The location for the next step is very important to some families. Some students just want to get away from home, but think about it first before you make a decision to move more than five hours away.

After you make your choice, prepare applications and start sending them off by the end of your junior year or over the summer break going into your senior year. Some applications will need essays and will cost a fee, but that is why you should do your research and narrow down your choices. I would suggest having your top five list and go from there. If you have a part-time job it would be a good idea to save as much money as you can while you still live at home. If you are already out on your own, then try to do a budget and put some money aside every time you get paid. You will need money for prom, graduation and yearbook pictures, trips and extra-curricular activities.

Short Term Goals

1.

2.

3.

_____

_____

_____

_____

_____

_____

_____

Long Term Goals

1.

_____

_____

_____

_____

2.

3.

Chapter 4 - 12th grade

Think about your Future

Senior year, you're thinking about prom, parties and graduation, but remember you still have important things to do this year. If you have not picked a school or an occupation to enter into after High School; this is the last and final year while in school, and as a minor, to make some important decisions about your future. Make sure you have all of your college applications filled out and turned in by the deadlines. Fill out your financial aid forms for the next year by the deadlines to ensure you receive all the aid you're entitled. Ask your guidance counselor about scholarships, if you do the right things it will be easier to pay for college. If you plan to go into the military, make sure you are exercising and fit, so that there will be no problems meeting the height and weight standards. If trade school is on your mind, then research programs that fit your interests. Most accredited schools offer financial aid. It is best to get into a program where you can obtain transfer credits, just in case you would like to attend another University after receiving an Associate's Degree. Communicate with your parents about deadlines, and if you do not know what the school requires, and you do not know where to find out information. **Do not be afraid to ask a teacher, a guidance counselor, or one of your peers. Now is the time to get help!**

Have fun! Be a teen while you have the chance. Play sports, go to dances, watch movies, but also finish your assignments, listen to your parents, respect your elders and learn from your mistakes. Remember no one is perfect, but if you learn to make good decisions, they can last a lifetime. If you have started dating by now and your parents have allowed it, then please be careful. Think about your future and what you want to accomplish, there will be time for committed relationships. Just don't miss out on being a teenager by trying to grow up too fast. It is ok to date and have fun, but it is also ok to wait to have sex. It is ok to make your future more of a priority than trying to settle down and rush into situations or relationships that you are really not ready for in High School. Find out who you are before committing yourself to being something for someone else. Of course, things happen in life, but just because someone you know has a baby in High School does not mean that is what you have to do. Being in a committed relationship with someone at this time, might not be the best thing if you are planning to move out of town. In some cases the relationship might hold you back from going where you want to go; and later you might resent the other person when things don't work out between you two. Enjoy your experience and live in the now. Believe me, you have the rest of your life to be an adult, pay bills, have kids, get married, work, etc.

The End of the Road

Now that you have made it this far, hopefully you have a little money saved. It is time to prepare to leave home in most cases to start your life as a young adult in your late teens. This might not be forever, but it is time for you to be responsible and be on your own. You want your parents to trust that you will make good decisions when there is peer pressure. You should treat people how you would want to be treated. Even though you think you know a lot, there is always more to learn.

Be humble and listen to people with experience that have good advice. You made it this far; do not follow the crowd now, stay focused. Some people did not make the right decisions and they do not want to see you succeed. You have to say to yourself "I will be successful" and think positively about achieving your goals, while telling yourself "I will achieve my goals." I would like all of you to start a **vision board**. A vision board can be on a big sheet of paper, but it can also be on a big three-fold cardboard. The vision board should consist of things you would like to achieve throughout your life. Think about what you would want most, which college or trade school you see yourself graduating from and put it on the board. You want to keep this board as many years as you can and add new goals as you get older. Look at the **vision board** from time to time to keep track of what you have achieved. If you do not motivate yourself, then who will? You have to want the best for yourself, and then go after your dream like someone was chasing you. This is your life and you have to make the best of it. Your mom and dad cannot accomplish your dreams for you, even if they help you along the way. It's time to make a difference in your own life, and then give back to others. **Be** confident, not conceited. **Be** strong, not a bully. **Be** humble, not arrogant. **Be** courageous, not afraid. **Be** the change, don't complain.

I just want to encourage the youth today, because you are our future leaders. Stand out from the crowd for something great. Don't be ashamed to succeed and don't be too prideful to help the next person achieve their goals. If you **get it**, help someone else **get it**, that's cool! **Being** smart is cool! **Being** a help is cool! **Being** a teen is cool! **Being** you is cool!

Short Term Goals

1.

_____

_____

2.

3.

_____

_____

_____

_____

_____

Long Term Goals

1.

_____

_____

_____

_____

_____

_____

_____

2.

_____

3.

About the Author: Monique Lynelle was born in Hartford, CT, and grew up mostly in Philadelphia, PA. She is the author of "My Journey at 30," as well as "A Teen's Guide to Succeed in High School." M.L. is a licensed cosmetologist and cosmetology instructor, and a 2012 graduate of Temple University. She also obtained an Associate's degree from Central Texas College while serving in the United States Army in 2008 and she is now a Veteran. Currently she attends Eastern University to obtain her Master's Degree, she is determined to overcome the obstacles that have come in her life and strives to complete her goals. Monique Lynelle is also a singer/songwriter, with a new song out called "Learning Me." She also was a semi-finalist of the "Hype Hair Magazine Natural Beauty Contest" in 2010 and 2011 and she competed in the "Big Beautiful Women's Pageant" in 2012. Throughout the years she has volunteered for various organizations. Monique Lynelle hopes to inspire people through her story and help bring out the best in others. Her motto is "Quitting is not an option."

Made in the USA
Charleston, SC
17 November 2012